HAL•LEONARD®

UKULELE PLAY-ALONG

AUDIO ACCESS INCLUDED

VOL. 38

JAZZ

Play 8 of Your Favorite Songs with Professional Audio Tracks

T0079175

Ukulele: Jay Brian Kummer
Production: Chris Kringel

PLAYBACK+
Speed • Pitch • Balance • Loop

To access audio visit:
www.halleonard.com/mylibrary

Enter Code
7896-6324-3075-0556

ISBN: 978-1-4950-0925-9

HAL•LEONARD®

Visit Hal Leonard Online at
www.halleonard.com

Contact Us:
Hal Leonard
7777 West Bluemound Road
Milwaukee, WI 53213
Email: info@halleonard.com

In Europe contact:
Hal Leonard Europe Limited
Distribution Centre, Newmarket Road
Bury St Edmunds, Suffolk, IP33 3YB
Email: info@halleonardeurope.com

In Australia contact:
Hal Leonard Australia Pty. Ltd.
4 Lentara Court
Cheltenham, Victoria, 3192 Australia
Email: info@halleonard.com.au

UKULELE NOTATION LEGEND

THE MUSICAL STAFF shows pitches and rhythms and is divided by bar lines into measures. Pitches are named after the first seven letters of the alphabet.

TABLATURE graphically represents the ukulele fingerboard. Each horizontal line represents a a string, and each number represents a fret.

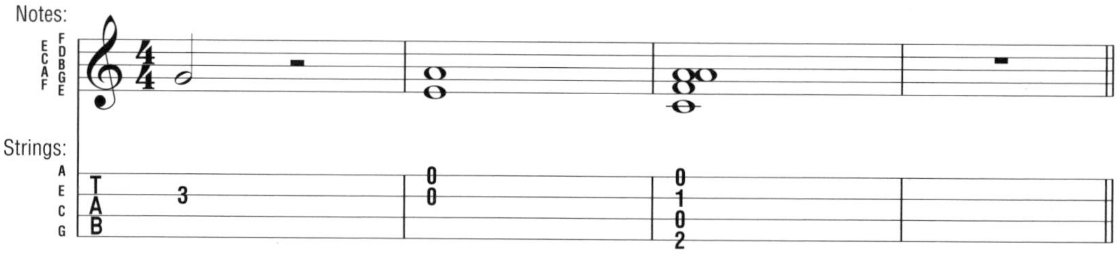

2nd string, 3rd fret

1st & 2nd strings open, played together

open F chord

HALF-STEP BEND: Strike the note and bend up 1/2 step.

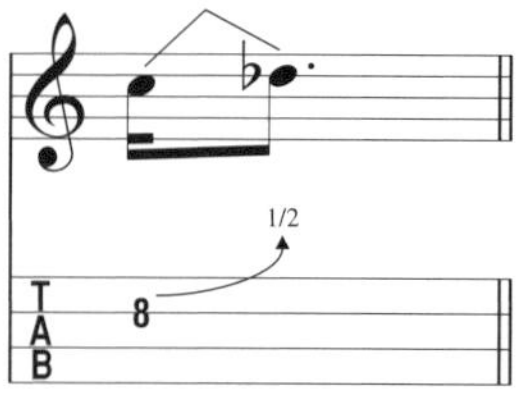

WHOLE-STEP BEND: Strike the note and bend up one step.

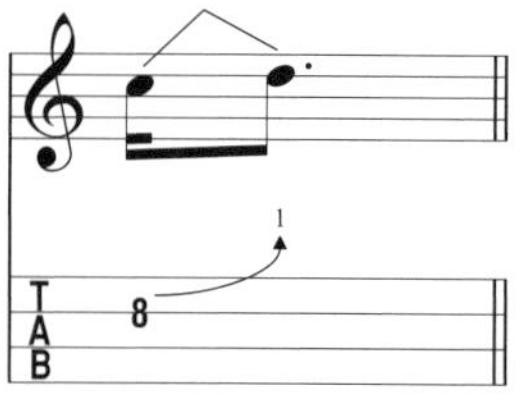

GRACE NOTE BEND: Strike the note and immediately bend up as indicated.

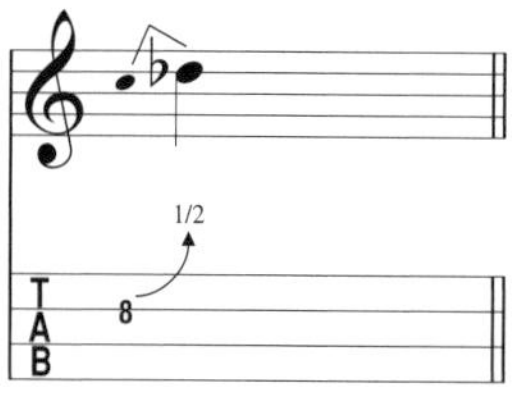

SLIGHT (MICROTONE) BEND: Strike the note and bend up 1/4 step.

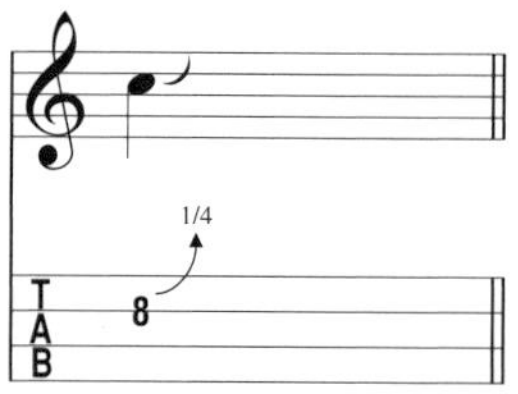

BEND AND RELEASE: Strike the note and bend up as indicated, then release back to the original note. Only the first note is struck.

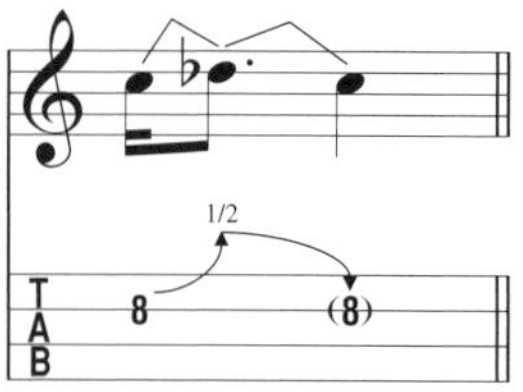

PRE-BEND: Bend the note as indicated, then strike it.

VIBRATO: The string is vibrated by rapidly bending and releasing the note with the fretting hand.

HAMMER-ON: Strike the first (lower) note with one finger, then sound the higher note (on the same string) with another finger by fretting it without picking.

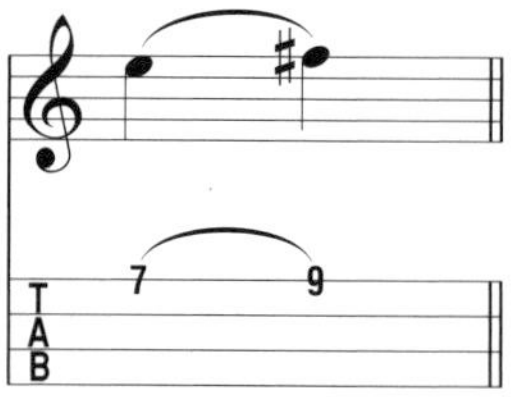

PULL-OFF: Place both fingers on the notes to be sounded. Strike the first note and without picking, pull the finger off to sound the second (lower) note.

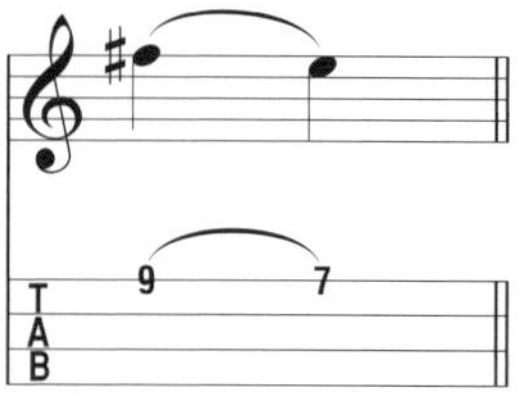

LEGATO SLIDE: Strike the first note and then slide the same fret-hand finger up or down to the second note. The second note is not struck.

SHIFT SLIDE: Same as legato slide, except the second note is struck.

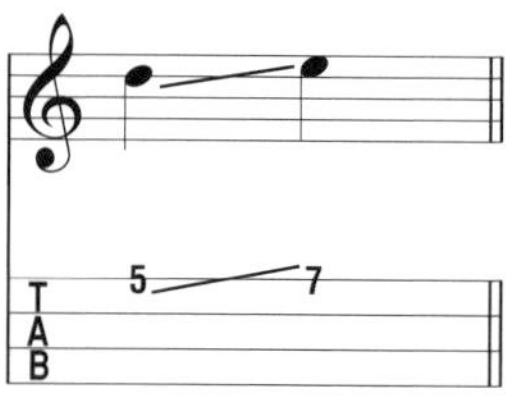

TRILL: Very rapidly alternate between the notes indicated by continuously hammering on and pulling off.

TREMOLO PICKING: The note is picked as rapidly and continuously as possible.

NOTE: Tablature numbers in parentheses mean:

1. The note is being sustained over a system (note in standard notation is tied), or
2. The note is sustained, but a new articulation (such as a hammer-on, pull-off, slide or vibrato) begins, or
3. The note is a barely audible "ghost" note (note in standard notation is also in parentheses).

Additional Musical Definitions

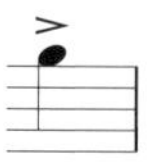

(accent) • Accentuate note (play it louder)

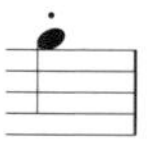

(staccato) • Play the note short

D.S. al Coda • Go back to the sign (𝄋), then play until the measure marked "***To Coda***," then skip to the section labelled "**Coda.**"

D.C. al Fine • Go back to the beginning of the song and play until the measure marked "***Fine***" (end).

N.C. • No chord.

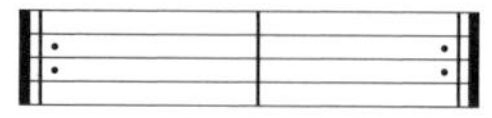

• Repeat measures between signs.

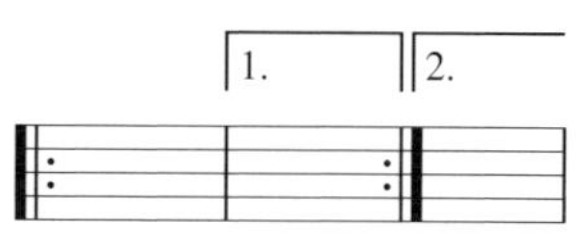

• When a repeated section has different endings, play the first ending only the first time and the second ending only the second time.

CONTENTS

After You've Gone

from ONE MO' TIME

Words by Henry Creamer
Music by Turner Layton

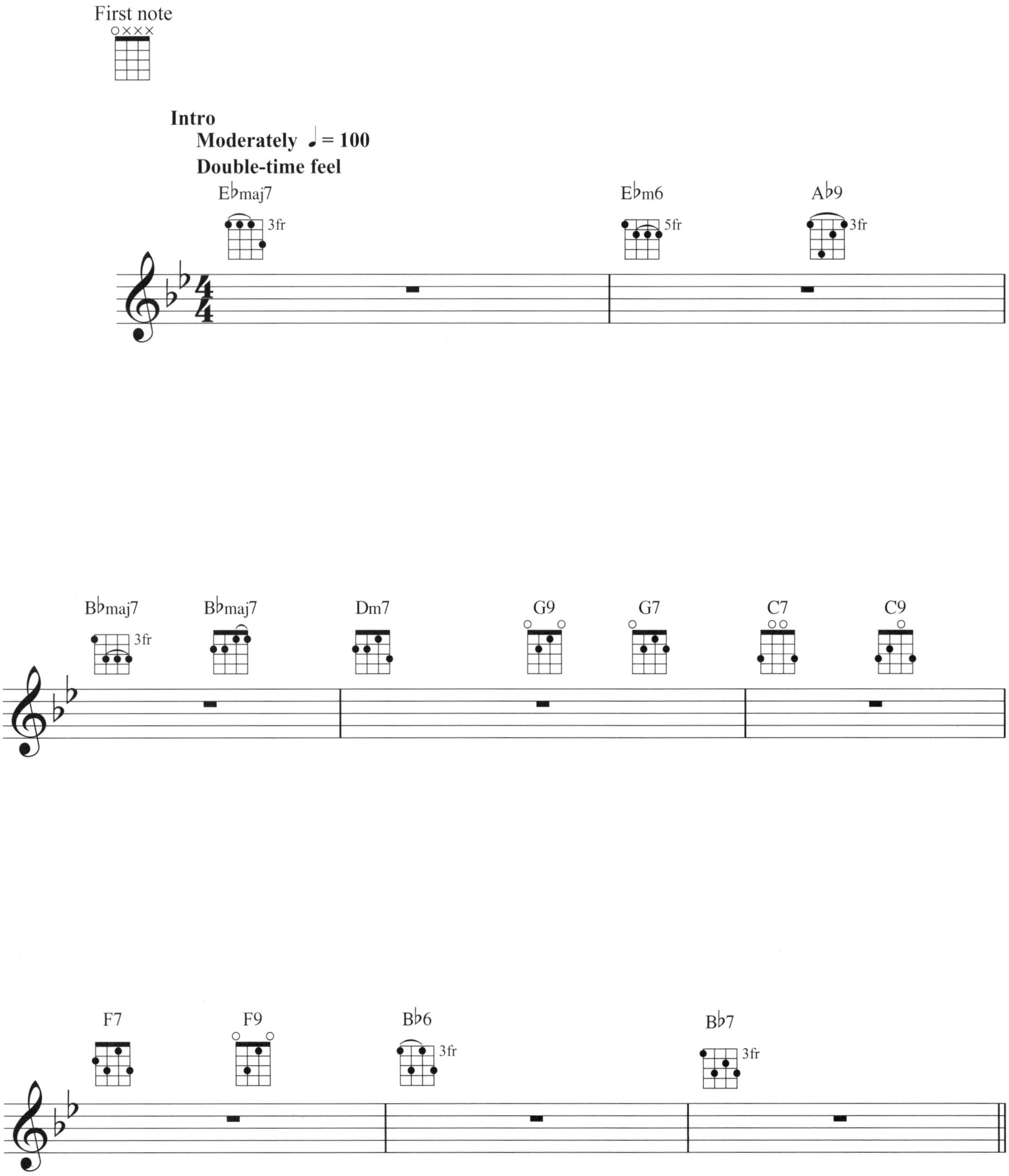

A
E♭maj7
3fr
E♭m6
5fr
A♭9
3fr
1. Af - ter you've gone, and left me cry - ing,
2. Instrumental
3. Af - ter I'm gone, af - ter we break up,
B♭maj7
3fr
B♭maj7
Dm7
G9
G7
af - ter you've gone, there's no de - ny - ing,
af - ter I'm gone, you're gon - na wake up,
C7
C9
F7
F9
you'll feel blue, you'll feel sad,
you will find you were blind
B♭6
3fr
B♭7
3fr
you'll miss the dear - est pal you've ev - er had.
to let some - bod - y come and change your mind.
B
E♭maj7
3fr
E♭m6
5fr
A♭9
3fr
There'll come a time, now don't for - get it,
Af - ter the years we've been to - geth - er,

B♭maj7 B♭maj7 Dm7 G9 G7
3fr
there'll come a time ___ when you'll re - gret it.
their joy and tears, ___ all kinds of weath - er.
Cm7 G7 Cm7 E♭m6 A♭9
5fr 3fr
Some day, when you grow lone - ly,
Some day, blue and down heart - ed,
B♭maj7 Am7 D7 Gm7 E°7
3fr 5fr 5fr 3fr 3fr
your heart will break like mine and you'll want me on - ly.
you'll long to be with me right back where you start - ed.
B♭6 G7 Cm7 F7
3fr
Aft - er you've gone, ___ af - ter you've gone a -
Aft - er I'm gone, ___ af - ter I'm gone a -
1., 2.
3.
B♭6 B♭7 B♭6
3fr 3fr 3fr
way. ___
way. ___

All the Things You Are

from VERY WARM FOR MAY

Lyrics by Oscar Hammerstein II
Music by Jerome Kern

Cm7 Fm7 Fm7 B♭7 B♭7 E♭maj7
4fr 3fr 3fr
You are the breath - less hush of eve - ning that
A♭maj7 Am7♭5 D7 Gmaj7 Gmaj7 E7 E7
7fr 7fr 4fr
trem - bles on the brink of a love - ly song. You are the
B
Am7 D7 D7 Gmaj7 Gmaj7
5fr 7fr
an - gel glow that lights a star. The dear - est
F♯m7♭5 F♯m7♭5 B7 B7 Emaj7 C7♯5
5fr 4fr 4fr
things I know are what you are.
C
Fm7 B♭m7 B♭m7 E♭7 E♭7 A♭maj7
6fr 6fr
Some day my hap - py arms will hold you, and
D♭maj7 G♭7 Cm7 B°7
3
some day I'll know that mo - ment di - vine, when

1., 2.
B♭m7
B♭m7
6fr
E♭7
6fr
E♭7
A♭maj7
Gm7♭5
C7♭9
all the things you
are are
mine.
3.
Outro
E♭7
6fr
E♭7
D♭7♯9
4fr
are are…
1., 2., 3.
C7♯9
3fr
4.
C7♯9
3fr

I Got Rhythm

from AN AMERICAN IN PARIS

Music and Lyrics by George Gershwin and Ira Gershwin

G7 C7 C7
mind him, you won't find him
C
F7 F7 B♭6 Gm7 Cm7 F7
'round my door. 3., 6. I got star - light,
Dm7 Gm7 Cm7 F7 B♭7 B♭7
I got sweet dreams, I got
To Coda
E♭7 E°7 B♭6 F7 B♭6
my man. Who could ask for an - y - thing more?
Solo
B♭6 Gm7 Cm7 F7 Dm7 Gm7 Cm7 F7
B♭7 B♭7 E♭7 E°7 B♭6 F7
1.
B♭6 F7

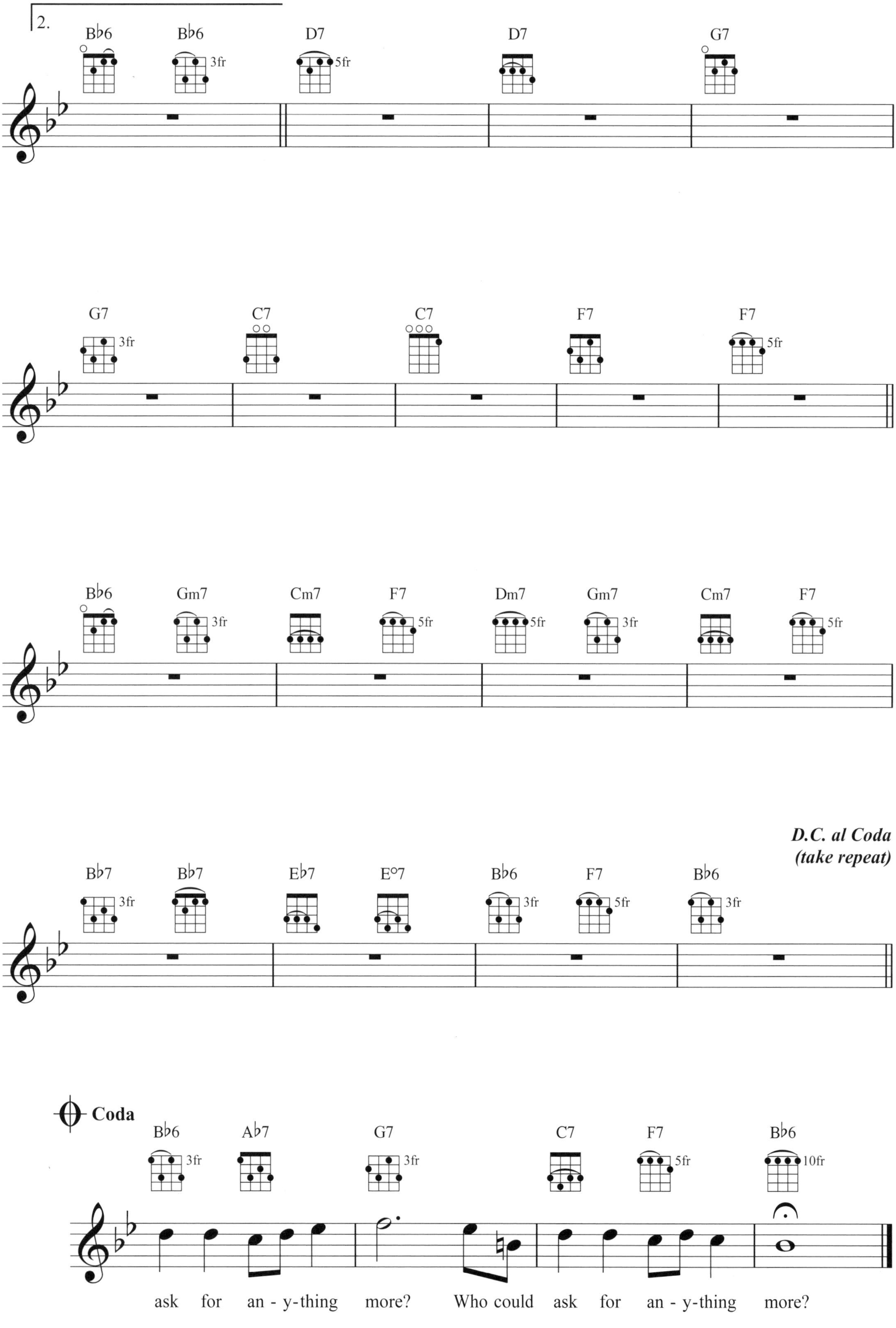
2.
B♭6 B♭6 3fr D7 5fr D7 G7
G7 3fr C7 C7 F7 F7 5fr
B♭6 Gm7 3fr Cm7 F7 5fr Dm7 5fr Gm7 3fr Cm7 F7 5fr
D.C. al Coda
(take repeat)
B♭7 3fr B♭7 E♭7 E°7 B♭6 3fr F7 5fr B♭6 3fr
Coda
B♭6 3fr A♭7 G7 3fr C7 F7 5fr B♭6 10fr
ask for an - y-thing more? Who could ask for an - y-thing more?

Is You Is, or Is You Ain't (Ma' Baby)

from FOLLOW THE BOYS

Words and Music by Billy Austin and Louis Jordan

B♭7 B♭7 E♭7 C7
want {her, him,} I'm gon-na ask {her: him:}
B
Fm C7 C7 Fm C7 C7 Fm
Is you is, or is you ain't ma' ba - by?
B7 B♭7 B♭m7 E♭7
The way you're act - ing late - ly makes me doubt.
A♭6 D♭7 C7 Fm C7 C7
You'se is
Fm C7 C7 Fm B7
still my ba - by, ba - by.
B♭7 B♭m7 E♭7 A♭6 E♭m7 A♭7
Seems my flame in your heart's done gone out.
1., 2. A

C
D♭maj7 D♭m7 A♭maj7
{woman is / man is just} a creature that has always been strange,
E♭m7 A♭7 D♭maj7 D♭m7 Cm7♭5 F7
just when you're sure of one you fine {she's / he's} gone and made a change.
D
B♭m7 Gm7♭5 C7 Fm C7 C7 Fm C7 C7
Is you is, or is you ain't ma' ba-
Fm B7 B♭7 B♭m7 E♭7
-by?
May-be ba-by's found some-bod-y new,
A♭6 G♭7♭5 F7 B♭7 B♭m7 E♭7
or is ma' ba-by still ma' ba-by true?
Outro
Repeat and fade
A♭6 A♭6 D♭7 C7 Fm D♭7 C7
3fr
4fr
5fr
6fr

Li'l Darlin'

By Neal Hefti

Dm7 G7 Gm7 C7 Am7 D7 D7
5fr 3fr 3fr 5fr 5fr
B
G9 G7 Dm7 D♭9 Gm7 Gm7 C7♭9 Am7 Am7
5fr 3fr 3fr 5fr
1., 2. Melody
D7 D7♭9 D7 D7 G9 G7 Dm7 D♭9 Gm7 Gm7 C7♭9
5fr 5fr 5fr 5fr 3fr 3fr
F7 F7♯5 B♭6 B♭m6 F7 F7
3fr 3fr 5fr
B♭6 B♭m6 Am7 D7♭9 D7 D7 G9 G7 Dm7 D♭9
3fr 3fr 5fr 5fr 5fr 3fr

Gm7 C7 C7♭9 F6 Am7 D7 D7
3fr
5fr
5fr
Outro
G9 G7 Dm7 D♭9 Gm7 C7 C7♭9 F6
5fr
3fr
3fr
Am7 D7 D7 G9 G7 Dm7 D♭9 Gm7 C7 C7♭9
5fr
5fr
5fr
3fr
3fr
F6 E♭m6 Dm7 D♭maj7 Gm11 Gm7 Gm7 Fmaj7
3fr
5fr
rit.

Lullaby of Birdland

Words by George David Weiss
Music by George Shearing

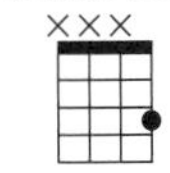

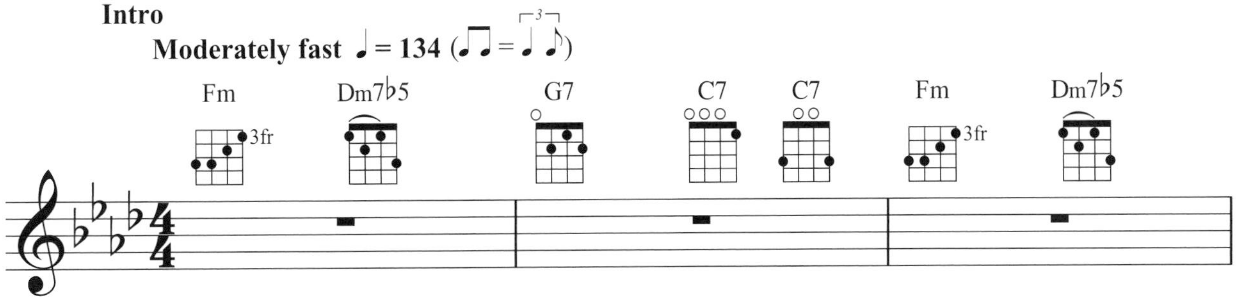

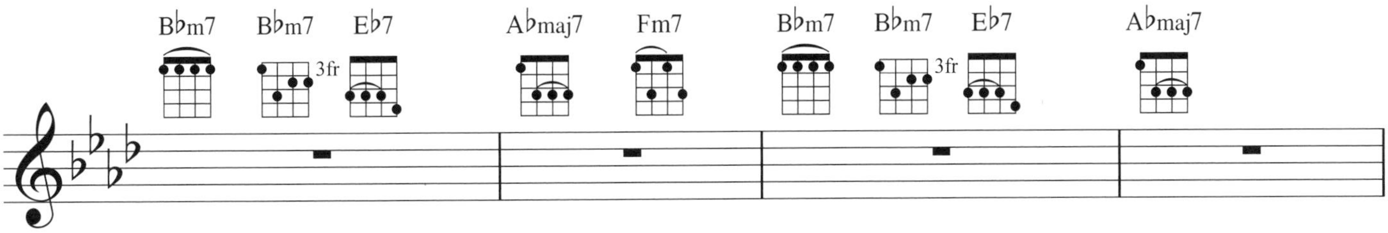

Fm Dm7♭5 B♭m7 B♭m7 E♭7 A♭maj7 Fm7
3fr
3fr
al - ways hear when you sigh. Nev - er in my world land could
bill and coo when they love? That's the kind of mag - ic mu -
1., 3., 5.
B♭m7 B♭m7 E♭7 A♭maj7 Gm7♭5 C7 C7
3fr
there be ways to re - veal, in a phrase, how I feel.
- sic we make with our lips
2., 4., 6.
B
A♭maj7 E♭7 A♭maj7 F7 F7 B♭m7 B♭m7
5fr
6fr
3fr
when we kiss.
1., 3. And there's a weep-y old wil - low,
2. Instrumental
B♭m7 E♭7 A♭maj7 F7 F7
5fr
he real - ly knows how to cry. That's how I'd cry in my pil -

B♭m7 B♭m7 B♭m7 E♭7 A♭maj7 C7 C7
6fr 3fr
- low ___ if you should tell me fare - well ___ and good - bye.
C
Fm Dm7♭5 G7 C7 C7 Fm Dm7♭5
3fr 3fr
1., 3. Lull - a - by of Bird - land, whis - per low, ___ kiss me sweet ___
2. Instrumental
B♭m7 E♭7 A♭maj7 Fm7 B♭m7 E♭7
and we'll go ___ fly - in' high in Bird - land high ___ in the sky ___ up a - bove, ___
1., 2.
D.S.
3.
A♭maj7 E♭7 A♭6 A♭maj7 E♭7 A♭6
___ we're in love. ___ we're in love.

Pick Yourself Up

from SWING TIME

Words by Dorothy Fields
Music by Jerome Kern

Em7 A7 D7sus4 D7 Bm7 E7
pleas - ant trip, and pick your-self up, dust your-self off,
C
Am7 D7 G6 A♭maj7 A♭6
start all o-ver a - gain. Work like a soul in - spi - red 'til the
E♭m7 A♭7 A♭7 Cmaj7 C6
bat-tle of the day is won. You may be sick and ti - red, but you'll
D
Am7 D7 Gm7 C7 Gm7 C7 Fmaj7 B♭maj7
be a man my son! Will you re-mem-ber the fa - mous men who
Em7♭5 A7 Dm7 G7 C7sus4 C7 Am7 D7
had to fall to rise a - gain? I pick my-self up, dust my-self off,
1. 2. 3.
Gm7 C7 F6 F6 N.C. F6
start all o-ver a gain. gain.

Take Five

By Paul Desmond

B
C♭maj7
4fr
B♭m7
A♭m7
4fr
G♭maj7
6fr
C♭maj7
4fr
B♭m7
3fr
A♭m7
Fm7♭5
B♭7♭9
C
E♭m
B♭m7
E♭m
B♭m7
E♭m
B♭m7

Ebm Bbm7 Ebm Bbm7 Ebm Bbm7
To Coda
Solo
Ebm Bbm7 Ebm Bbm7 Ebm Bbm7
Ebm Bbm7 Ebm Bbm7 Ebm Bbm7 Ebm Bbm7
Ebm Bbm7 Ebm Bbm7 Ebm Bbm7 Cbmaj7
Bbm7 Abm7 Gbmaj7 Cbmaj7 Bbm7
Abm7 Fm7b5 Bb7b9 Ebm Bbm7 Ebm Bbm7

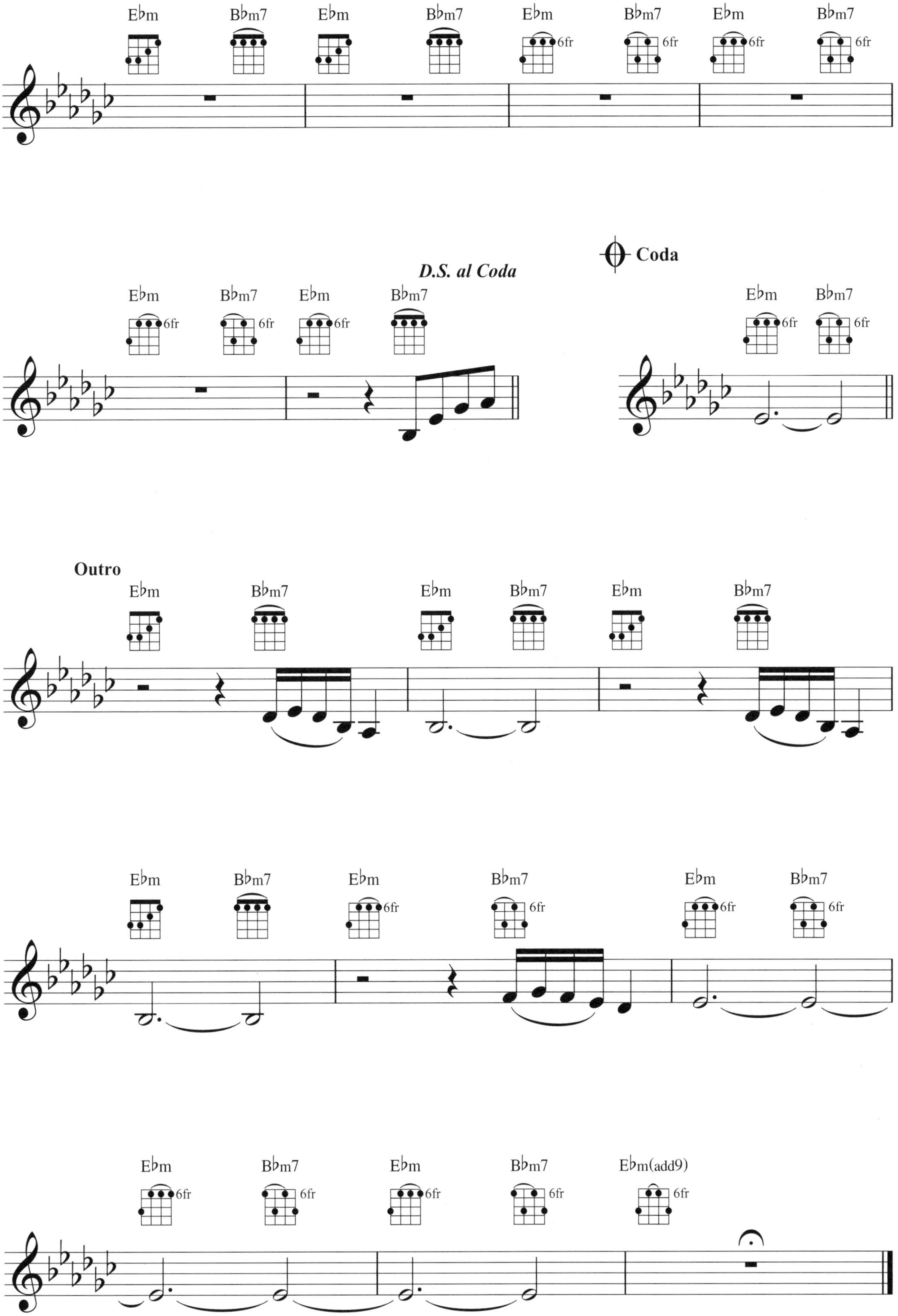
E♭m B♭m7 E♭m B♭m7 E♭m B♭m7 E♭m B♭m7
6fr
D.S. al Coda
Coda
E♭m B♭m7 E♭m B♭m7
Outro
E♭m B♭m7 E♭m B♭m7 E♭m B♭m7
E♭m B♭m7 E♭m B♭m7 E♭m B♭m7
E♭m B♭m7 E♭m B♭m7 E♭m(add9)

Ride the Ukulele Wave!

The Beach Boys for Ukulele

This folio features 20 favorites, including: Barbara Ann • Be True to Your School • California Girls • Fun, Fun, Fun • God Only Knows • Good Vibrations • Help Me Rhonda • I Get Around • In My Room • Kokomo • Little Deuce Coupe • Sloop John B • Surfin' U.S.A. • Wouldn't It Be Nice • and more!

00701726 . . . . $14.99

Disney Songs for Ukulele

20 great Disney classics arranged for all uke players, including: Beauty and the Beast • Bibbidi-Bobbidi-Boo (The Magic Song) • Can You Feel the Love Tonight • Chim Chim Cher-ee • Heigh-Ho • It's a Small World • Some Day My Prince Will Come • We're All in This Together • When You Wish upon a Star • and more.

00701708 . . . . $14.99

Jack Johnson – Strum & Sing

Cherry Lane Music

Strum along with 41 Jack Johnson songs using this top-notch collection of chords and lyrics just for the uke! Includes: Better Together • Bubble Toes • Cocoon • Do You Remember • Flake • Fortunate Fool • Good People • Holes to Heaven • Taylor • Tomorrow Morning • and more.

02501702 . . . . $17.99

The Beatles for Ukulele

Ukulele players can strum, sing and pick along with 20 Beatles classics! Includes: All You Need Is Love • Eight Days a Week • Good Day Sunshine • Here, There and Everywhere • Let It Be • Love Me Do • Penny Lane • Yesterday • and more.

00700154 . . . . $16.99

First 50 Songs You Should Play on Ukulele

An amazing collection of 50 accessible, must-know favorites: Edelweiss • Hey, Soul Sister • I Walk the Line • I'm Yours • Imagine • Over the Rainbow • Peaceful Easy Feeling • The Rainbow Connection • Riptide • and many more.

00149250 . . . . $14.99

Elvis Presley for Ukulele

arr. Jim Beloff

20 classic hits from The King: All Shook Up • Blue Hawaii • Blue Suede Shoes • Can't Help Falling in Love • Don't • Heartbreak Hotel • Hound Dog • Jailhouse Rock • Love Me • Love Me Tender • Return to Sender • Suspicious Minds • Teddy Bear • and more.

00701004 . . . . $15.99

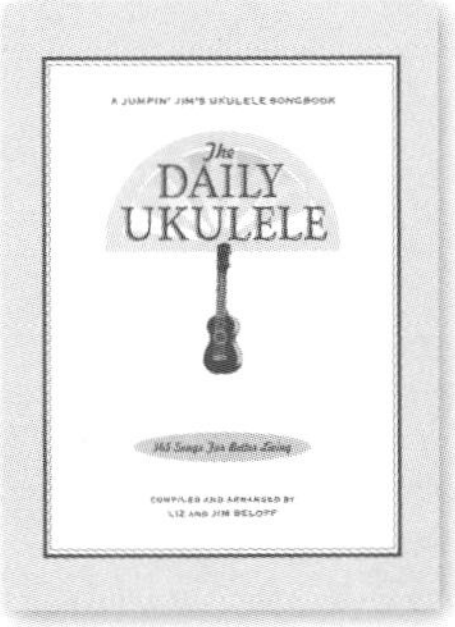

The Daily Ukulele

compiled and arranged by

Liz and Jim Beloff

Strum a different song everyday with easy arrangements of 365 of your favorite songs in one big songbook! Includes favorites by the Beatles, Beach Boys, and Bob Dylan, folk songs, pop songs, kids' songs, Christmas carols, and Broadway and Hollywood tunes, all with a spiral binding for ease of use.

00240356 . . . . $39.99

Folk Songs for Ukulele

A great collection to take along to the campfire! 60 folk songs, including: Amazing Grace • Buffalo Gals • Camptown Races • For He's a Jolly Good Fellow • Good Night Ladies • Home on the Range • I've Been Working on the Railroad • Kumbaya • My Bonnie Lies over the Ocean • On Top of Old Smoky • Scarborough Fair • Swing Low, Sweet Chariot • Take Me Out to the Ball Game • Yankee Doodle • and more.

00696068 . . . . $12.99

Jake Shimabukuro – Peace Love Ukulele

Deemed "the Hendrix of the ukulele," Hawaii native Jake Shimabukuro is a uke virtuoso. Our songbook features note-for-note transcriptions with ukulele tablature of Jake's masterful playing on all the CD tracks: Bohemian Rhapsody • Boy Meets Girl • Bring Your Adz • Hallelujah • Pianoforte 2010 • Variation on a Dance 2010 • and more, plus two bonus selections!

00702516 . . . . $19.99

The Daily Ukulele – Leap Year Edition

366 More Songs for Better Living

compiled and arranged by

Liz and Jim Beloff

An amazing second volume with 366 MORE songs for you to master each day of a leap year! Includes: Ain't No Sunshine • Calendar Girl • I Got You Babe • Lean on Me • Moondance • and many, many more.

00240681 . . . . $39.99

Hawaiian Songs for Ukulele

Over thirty songs from the state that made the ukulele famous, including: Beyond the Rainbow • Hanalei Moon • Ka-lu-a • Lovely Hula Girl • Mele Kalikimaka • One More Aloha • Sea Breeze • Tiny Bubbles • Waikiki • and more.

00696065 . . . . $10.99

Worship Songs for Ukulele

25 worship songs: Amazing Grace (My Chains are Gone) • Blessed Be Your Name • Enough • God of Wonders • Holy Is the Lord • How Great Is Our God • In Christ Alone • Love the Lord • Mighty to Save • Sing to the King • Step by Step • We Fall Down • and more.

00702546 . . . . $14.99

UKULELE CHORD SONGBOOKS

This series features convenient 6" x 9" books with complete lyrics and chord symbols for dozens of great songs. Each song also includes chord grids at the top of every page and the first notes of the melody for easy reference.

ACOUSTIC ROCK

60 tunes: American Pie • Band on the Run • Catch the Wind • Daydream • Every Rose Has Its Thorn • Hallelujah • Iris • More Than Words • Patience • The Sound of Silence • Space Oddity • Sweet Talkin' Woman • Wake up Little Susie • Who'll Stop the Rain • and more.
00702482 . . . . $14.99

THE BEATLES

100 favorites: Across the Universe • Carry That Weight • Dear Prudence • Good Day Sunshine • Here Comes the Sun • If I Fell • Love Me Do • Michelle • Ob-La-Di, Ob-La-Da • Revolution • Something • Ticket to Ride • We Can Work It Out • and many more.
00703065 . . . . $19.99

BEST SONGS EVER

70 songs: All I Ask of You • Bewitched • Edelweiss • Just the Way You Are • Let It Be • Memory • Moon River • Over the Rainbow • Someone to Watch over Me • Unchained Melody • You Are the Sunshine of My Life • You Raise Me Up • and more.
00117050 . . . . $16.99

CHILDREN'S SONGS

80 classics: Alphabet Song • "C" Is for Cookie • Do-Re-Mi • I'm Popeye the Sailor Man • Mickey Mouse March • Oh! Susanna • Polly Wolly Doodle • Puff the Magic Dragon • The Rainbow Connection • Sing • Three Little Fishies (Itty Bitty Poo) • and many more.
00702473 . . . . $14.99

CHRISTMAS CAROLS

75 favorites: Away in a Manger • Coventry Carol • The First Noel • Good King Wenceslas • Hark! the Herald Angels Sing • I Saw Three Ships • Joy to the World • O Little Town of Bethlehem • Still, Still, Still • Up on the Housetop • What Child Is This? • and more.
00702474 . . . . $14.99

CHRISTMAS SONGS

55 Christmas classics: Do They Know It's Christmas? • Frosty the Snow Man • Happy Xmas (War Is Over) • Jingle-Bell Rock • Little Saint Nick • The Most Wonderful Time of the Year • White Christmas • and more.
00101776 . . . . $14.99

ISLAND SONGS

60 beach party tunes: Blue Hawaii • Day-O (The Banana Boat Song) • Don't Worry, Be Happy • Island Girl • Kokomo • Lovely Hula Girl • Mele Kalikimaka • Red, Red Wine • Surfer Girl • Tiny Bubbles • Ukulele Lady • and many more.
00702471 . . . . $16.99

150 OF THE MOST BEAUTIFUL SONGS EVER

150 melodies: Always • Bewitched • Candle in the Wind • Endless Love • In the Still of the Night • Just the Way You Are • Memory • The Nearness of You • People • The Rainbow Connection • Smile • Unchained Melody • What a Wonderful World • Yesterday • and more.
00117051 . . . . $24.99

PETER, PAUL & MARY

Over 40 songs: And When I Die • Blowin' in the Wind • Goodnight, Irene • If I Had a Hammer (The Hammer Song) • Leaving on a Jet Plane • Puff the Magic Dragon • This Land Is Your Land • We Shall Overcome • Where Have All the Flowers Gone? • and more.
00121822 . . . . $12.99

THREE CHORD SONGS

60 songs: Bad Case of Loving You • Bang a Gong (Get It On) • Blue Suede Shoes • Cecilia • Get Back • Hound Dog • Kiss • Me and Bobby McGee • Not Fade Away • Rock This Town • Sweet Home Chicago • Twist and Shout • You Are My Sunshine • and more.
00702483 . . . . $14.99

TOP HITS

31 hits: The A Team • Born This Way • Forget You • Ho Hey • Jar of Hearts • Little Talks • Need You Now • Rolling in the Deep • Teenage Dream • Titanium • We Are Never Ever Getting Back Together • and more.
00115929 . . . . $14.99

Prices, contents, and availability subject to change without notice.

HAL•LEONARD®

www.halleonard.com

Learn To Play Today with folk music instruction from

HAL•LEONARD®

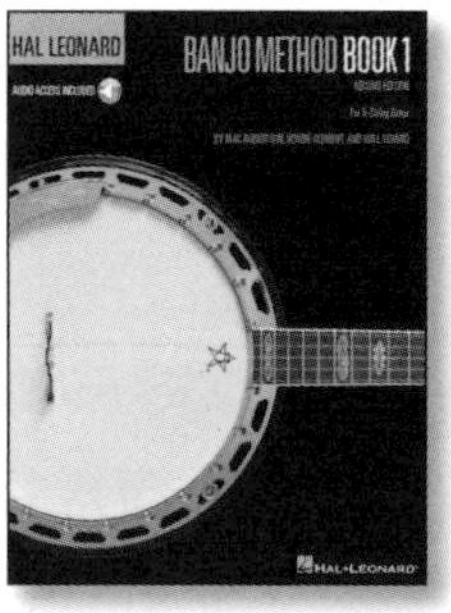

Hal Leonard Banjo Method – Second Edition

Authored by Mac Robertson, Robbie Clement & Will Schmid. This innovative method teaches 5-string, bluegrass style. The method consists of two instruction books and two cross-referenced supplement books that offer the beginner a carefully-paced and interest-keeping approach to the bluegrass style.

Method Book 1
00699500 Book $7.99
00695101 Book/Online Audio $16.99

Method Book 2
00699502 .... $7.99

Supplementary Songbooks
00699515 Easy Banjo Solos $9.99
00699516 More Easy Banjo Solos $9.99

Hal Leonard Dulcimer Method – Second Edition

by Neal Hellman

A beginning method for the Appalachian dulcimer with a unique new approach to solo melody and chord playing. Includes tuning, modes and many beautiful folk songs all demonstrated on the audio accompaniment. Music and tablature.
00699289 Book $9.99
00697230 Book/Online Audio $16.99

The Hal Leonard Complete Harmonica Method – Chromatic Harmonica

by Bobby Joe Holman

The only harmonica method to present the chromatic harmonica in 14 scales and modes in all 12 keys!
00841286 Book/Online Audio $12.99

The Hal Leonard Complete Harmonica Method – The Diatonic Harmonica

by Bobby Joe Holman

This terrific method book/CD pack specific to the diatonic harmonica covers all six positions! It contains more than 20 songs and musical examples.
00841285 Book/Online Audio $12.99

Hal Leonard Fiddle Method

by Chris Wagoner

The Hal Leonard Fiddle Method is the perfect introduction to playing folk, bluegrass and country styles on the violin. Many traditional tunes are included to illustrate a variety of techniques. The accompanying audio includes many tracks for demonstration and play-along. Covers: instrument selection and care; playing positions; theory; slides & slurs; shuffle feel; bowing; drones; playing "backup"; cross-tuning; and much more!
00311415 Book $6.99
00311416 Book/Online Audio $10.99

The Hal Leonard Mandolin Method – Second Edition

Noted mandolinist and teacher Rich Del Grosso has authored this excellent mandolin method that features great playable tunes in several styles (bluegrass, country, folk, blues) in standard music notation and tablature. The audio features play-along duets.
00699296 Book $7.99
00695102 Book/Online Audio $15.99

Hal Leonard Oud Method

by John Bilezikjian

This book teaches the fundamentals of standard Western music notation in the context of oud playing. It also covers: types of ouds, tuning the oud, playing position, how to string the oud, scales, chords, arpeggios, tremolo technique, studies and exercises, songs and rhythms from Armenia and the Middle East, and 25 audio tracks for demonstration and play along.
00695836 Book/Online Audio $12.99

Hal Leonard Ukulele Method Book 1

INCLUDES TAB

by Lil' Rev

This comprehensive and easy-to-use beginner's guide by acclaimed performer and uke master Lil' Rev includes many fun songs of different styles to learn and play. Includes: types of ukuleles, tuning, music reading, melody playing, chords, strumming, scales, tremolo, music notation and tablature, a variety of music styles, ukulele history and much more.
00695847 Book $6.99
00695832 Book/Online Audio $10.99

HAL•LEONARD®

Visit Hal Leonard Online at
www.halleonard.com

Prices and availability subject to change without notice.